Looking at...Protoceratops
A Dinosaur from the CRETACEOUS Period

For a free color catalog describing Gareth Stevens's list of high-quality books, call 1-800-341-3569 (USA) or 1-800-461-9120 (Canada).

ISBN 0-8368-1046-5

This North American edition first published in 1993 by
Gareth Stevens Publishing
1555 North RiverCenter Drive, Suite 201
Milwaukee, Wisconsin 53212 USA

This U.S. edition © 1993 by Gareth Stevens, Inc. Created with original
© 1993 by Quartz Editorial Services, Premier House, 112 Station Road,
Edgware HA8 7AQ U.K.

Consultant: Dr. David Norman, Director of the Sedgwick Museum of Geology,
University of Cambridge, England.

Printed in MEXICO
1 2 3 4 5 6 7 8 9 98 97 96 95 94 93

At this time, Gareth Stevens, Inc., does not use 100 percent recycled paper, although the paper
used in our books does contain about 30 percent recycled fiber. This decision was made after a
careful study of current recycling procedures revealed their dubious environmental benefits. We
will continue to explore recycling options.

Looking at...Protoceratops
A Dinosaur from the CRETACEOUS Period

by **Heather Amery**

Illustrated by **Tony Gibbons**

THE NEW
DINOSAUR
COLLECTION

Gareth Stevens Publishing
MILWAUKEE

Contents

Introducing
Protoceratops

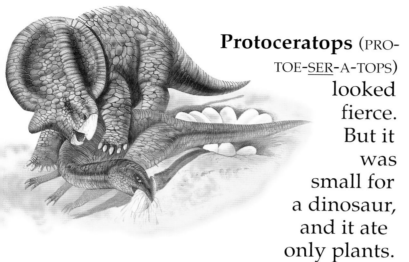

Protoceratops (PRO-TOE-SER-A-TOPS) looked fierce. But it was small for a dinosaur, and it ate only plants.

This dinosaur lived millions of years ago in Late Cretaceous times, wandering around in peaceful herds of several families and feeding on tough, woody plants. The females laid eggs, guarding them until they hatched.

From its skeleton, we know that **Protoceratops** had a beaked mouth, somewhat like a turtle's, and a large, bony frill around the back of its neck.

With a heavy, clumsy body, it stumped along on four sturdy legs, holding up its thick tail.

Where did scientists first find **Protoceratops?** How did it watch over its eggs? What do we now know about this strange creature?

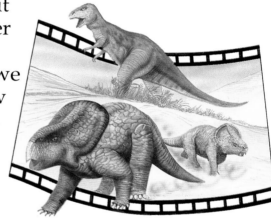

Could **Protoceratops** fight off the meat-eating dinosaurs? Did it use the frill around its neck as a weapon, or was this just for show?

Read about one of the most interesting dinosaurs of all as you turn the following pages.

Frilled creature

Protoceratops was a squat, clumsy-looking dinosaur that lived in what is now the Gobi Desert in Mongolia, Asia.

About as long as a bed and only as high as your waist, it plodded along on four stumpy legs.

It had a big head with a bony frill around its neck. This made it look fierce and dangerous. And it may well have scared you, if you had suddenly come face to face with it. But, of course, there were no humans around about 100 million years ago. And **Protoceratops** probably did not fight unless attacked.

There were bumps, like horns, on **Protoceratops's** head. But these horns were really tiny when compared with the much larger horns of such dinosaurs as **Triceratops** (TRY-SER-A-TOPS).

6

Protoceratops bit off vegetation with its horned beak, which was curved like a parrot's. Then, it crunched up its food between the rows of short, blunt teeth at the back of its jaws.

Although Protoceratops had no teeth at the front of its mouth, it could have given an enemy a nasty bite with its beak.

Its enemies were large meat-eaters like **Tarbosaurus** (TAR-BO-SAW-RUS), who thought **Protoceratops** would make a good meal.

Another tool for fighting against predators was **Protoceratops's** large, thick tail. This was almost as long as its body. It may have used the tail to strike at its enemies with violent sideways blows. This would have wounded enemies and stopped their attacks.

Protoceratops's head frill would also have been useful in times of danger, protecting its body like a shield.

The frill provided an anchor for strong jaw muscles, too. But it was not as heavy as it looks because there were large openings in the bone at its back edge.

Adult males probably had frills that were more upright than those of female **Protoceratops.** Scientists believe the males also may have had larger snouts. These larger frills and snouts may have made the males more attractive to females.

Small but powerful

Protoceratops had a skeleton of strong, thick bone to hold up the weight of its bulky body, which was heavy for its small size. Most **Protoceratops** were no bigger than large dogs.

Scientists believe **Protoceratops** walked mainly on all fours. But it may have been able to balance on its hind legs.

Notice how the back legs of **Protoceratops** were much longer than the front legs.

Protoceratops could probably run fast when in danger, but it was usually satisfied to slowly lumber along.

8

The skeletons of the males were probably much larger than those of the females. **Protoceratops** skeletons also seem to have had differently shaped frills around their necks. Frills belonging to the males were probably bigger, too, just as their bodies were.

Take a look at the size of **Protoceratops's** head. It was about half the length of its body, without the tail.

There were no teeth at the front of the beak, which was made of hard bone.

Protoceratops's jaws had strong muscles that helped it chew plants. It also had powerful muscles linked to the neck frill that were used for holding up its head. As it moved, **Protoceratops** held its head up level with its body and tail.

The frill was like a round, flat collar and was made of solid bone. It spread out backward from the skull. The bone had two large holes in it to make it lighter.

Thousands of years ago, when the Chinese found bones and teeth like those of this skeleton, they thought they belonged to dragons.

Protoceratops had an unusual mouth shaped like a curved beak. The top jaw was longer than the lower jaw.

But, of course, dragons never really existed. We now know that they were the bones of dinosaurs, such as **Protoceratops**.

Protoceratops discovered

About 70 years ago, a group of scientists from the American Museum of Natural History went on an expedition to the Gobi Desert in Mongolia.

They were hoping to find proof that the first human beings had lived there and to learn something about them.

After many months of exploration, the scientists found nothing. Then, suddenly, they made a very exciting discovery.

In an area that is called Flaming Cliffs because of the red color of its rocks, the explorers came across many fossilized dinosaur nests filled with eggs – the first that had ever been found.

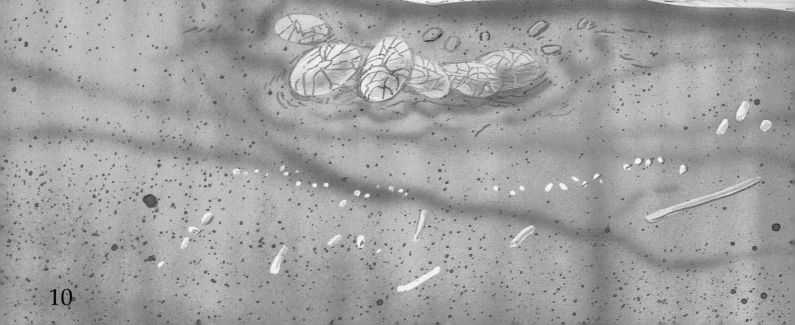

Near the nests were many bones that seemed to come from a strange dinosaur with a frill around its neck. They named it **Protoceratops**.

They also found the fossilized bones of tiny, newly hatched dinosaurs, babies still in the eggs, and hundreds of pieces of eggshell.

The scientists had accidentally stumbled across something very special – the first dinosaur eggs ever to be found.

Until this discovery, scientists had not known for certain if dinosaurs hatched out of eggs, like reptiles, or if the young were born alive.

Life with Protoceratops

Protoceratops lived in family groups in the Gobi Desert in Mongolia.

Millions of years ago, the weather was warm with no cold winters, and the plants and trees grew quickly.

Each year, at the beginning of the mating season, the males in each **Protoceratops** herd fought each other for females. Then, they would mate.

The females laid eggs. Once the young had hatched, the females also guarded them. Later, when the babies were old enough, the herd may have moved to find fresh feeding grounds.

There were giant, meat-eating dinosaurs that would attack **Protoceratops**, too. **Tarbosaurus**, for example, was as long as three cars and nearly as tall as a giraffe.

Tarbosaurus had a huge mouth with long, sharp teeth. Even the biggest and strongest **Protoceratops** was no match for this huge predator.

As they ate, they had to watch out for danger. There were many small dinosaurs that would try to steal **Protoceratops** eggs or snatch a baby.

This is why it was important for **Protoceratops** to stay together in the herd.

13

Leader of the pack

Herds of **Protoceratops** roamed the plains of Mongolia about 100 million years ago.

Like herds of deer or elephants today, they lived in peaceful family groups for most of the year.

But, at the start of the mating season, scientists think that a young male would challenge the old leader to see who would lead the herd next.

Standing a few feet (m) apart, they would roar fiercely at one another. Then, they charged, butting each other with their bony heads, giving powerful sideways blows with their frills, and slapping their tails.

The battle might last just for a few minutes or much longer.

When, at last, the weaker animal was exhausted, it walked away. It may have been battered and bruised but was probably not seriously wounded. It now took its place in the herd again until the next mating season. The victor would be the new leader of the herd.

15

Dinosaur nursery

Near Flaming Cliffs in the Gobi Desert, a herd of **Protoceratops** stopped to lay their eggs. The mothers used their feet to scrape out round nests in the sandy soil.

When a nest was ready, a mother would carefully drop each egg in the nest in a neat spiral. When she had laid about 12 eggs, the mother plodded away to leave room for another mother to lay her eggs in the same, shared nest. The eggs of several mothers would hatch in one nest.

16

Nearby, there would have been other **Protoceratops** nests with up to 30 eggs in each. **Protoceratops** mothers probably covered their eggs with sand to keep them warm.

Instead of sitting on the nests, they relied on the Sun's heat to incubate the eggs. The eggs were about 8 inches (20 cm) long and shaped like fat sausages. The tough, wrinkly shells protected the growing babies curled up inside from being crushed or drying out.

When the baby **Protoceratops** hatched out of their shells, each one was only about 12 inches (30 cm) long.

The mothers probably brought them food and guarded them against such meat-eating, or carnivorous, dinosaurs as **Tarbosaurus**.

Soon, the babies would be old enough and strong enough to look after themselves.

Many **Protoceratops** nests have been found very well preserved.

On guard!

A **Protoceratops** mother lay on the sandy ground, resting by her nest in the heat of the day. The Sun was helping incubate her eggs. They would soon hatch.

But there were dinosaur egg thieves around that might possibly steal and eat the eggs.

Oviraptor (OVE-IH-RAP-TOR), for instance, was a small dinosaur with strong, three-fingered hands. Its name means "egg-stealer." It had strong jaws and a bony beak that could easily crack a shell even though it had no teeth.

But **Oviraptor** would have thought twice about attacking an adult **Protoceratops**. This dinosaur had such a tough, well-armored body that **Oviraptor** would have stood little chance of hurting it. **Oviraptor** knew that its best chance of having a dinosaur for dinner was if it could gets its hands on a baby or steal some eggs.

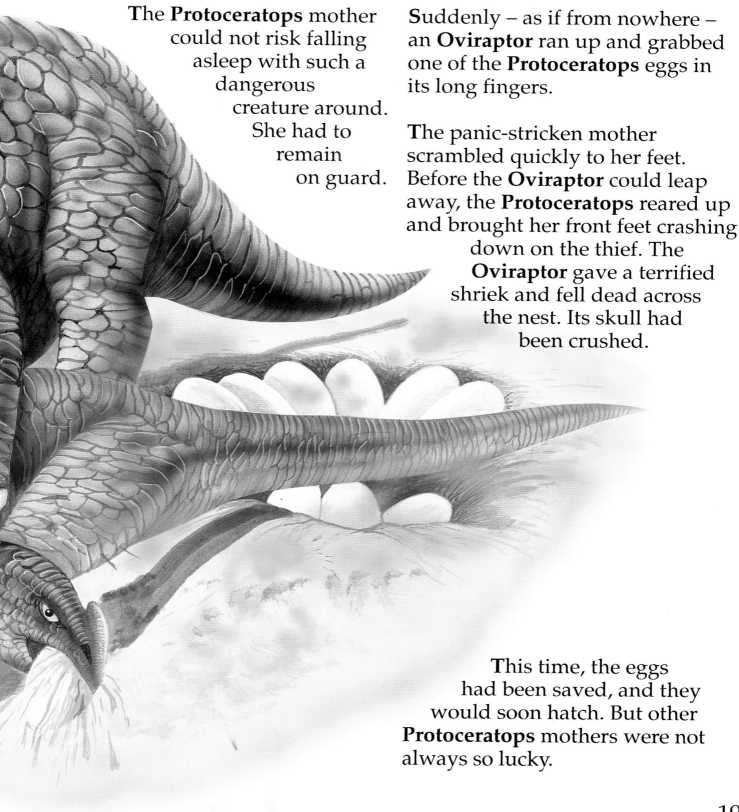

The **Protoceratops** mother could not risk falling asleep with such a dangerous creature around. She had to remain on guard.

Suddenly – as if from nowhere – an **Oviraptor** ran up and grabbed one of the **Protoceratops** eggs in its long fingers.

The panic-stricken mother scrambled quickly to her feet. Before the **Oviraptor** could leap away, the **Protoceratops** reared up and brought her front feet crashing down on the thief. The **Oviraptor** gave a terrified shriek and fell dead across the nest. Its skull had been crushed.

This time, the eggs had been saved, and they would soon hatch. But other **Protoceratops** mothers were not always so lucky.

Protoceratops data

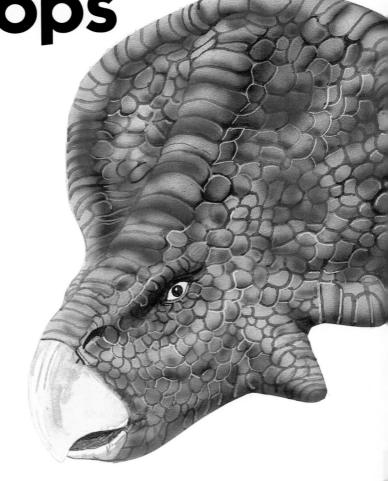

Protoceratops was a small, bulky dinosaur. It had a big head with a frilly collar and a bumpy snout. Walking heavily on all four legs, it probably swayed its thick tail from side to side as it searched for fresh plants to eat.

Parrotlike beak

Protoceratops had no teeth at the front of its mouth. Instead, it had a bony beak shaped very much like a parrot's. At the back of its jaws, it had rows of teeth for grinding all the tough leaves and plants it plucked with its beak.

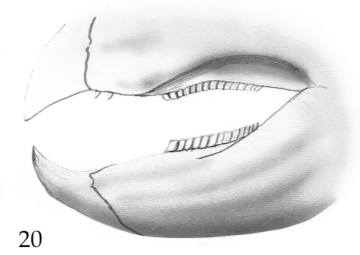

Frilly collar

Protoceratops had a big, bony frill around its neck. This acted like a shield, protecting it from the claws and teeth of the meat-eating dinosaurs that attacked it. The frills of the males may have been bigger than those of the females. The males may also have used their frills to signal the rest of the herd at the start of the mating season.

Bony head

Protoceratops had a big, heavy head with bony bumps on its nose. It also had bumps over its eyes. Scientists think **Protoceratops** must have used its strong skull for butting and pushing other members of its herd when fighting for leadership.

Clawed feet

Protoceratops's feet were broad and strong. There were four toes with short claws on each foot. They were probably too short to be useful for fighting, but they may have helped **Protoceratops** get a grip on slippery ground. The females would also have used these claws when scraping out their nests.

Thick tail

Almost as long as its body, **Protoceratops's** tail was thick and powerful. **Protoceratops** probably held it up when running. A single sideways blow with its tail would easily have broken the leg of a small attacking dinosaur. **Protoceratops** may also have used its tail in a swishing movement to ward off a challenge from another male.

The Protoceratopsid family

Protoceratops belonged to a dinosaur family, or group, called **Protoceratopsids.** There were several different branches of this group that lived in different parts of the world. They were small dinosaurs with bony lumps on their noses and frills around their necks.

1

3

Protoceratops (1), with a name meaning "first horned face," was the earliest dinosaur known to have lumps, like very small horns, on its head. It roamed in herds and ate plants and trees.

Montanaceratops (MON-TANNA-SER-A-TOPS) **(2)** was a cousin of **Protoceratops** and was about twice as long.

Montanaceratops means "horned face from Montana."

Bagaceratops (BAG-A-SER-A-TOPS) **(3)** was a smaller member of the family. Like the others, it had a neck frill, a parrotlike beak, and a nose horn. Its name means "small horned face."

Microceratops (MY-CRO-SER-A-TOPS) **(4)** was another relative. It is also one of the smallest dinosaurs ever found.

2

4

GLOSSARY

butt — to push or strike with horns or the head.

expedition — a journey or voyage.

fossils — traces or remains of plants and animals found in rock.

frill — a fringe or ruffle around the neck of an animal.

herbivores — plant-eating animals.

herd — a group of animals that travels and lives together.

mate — to join together (animals) to produce young.

predators — animals that kill other animals for food.

reptiles — cold-blooded animals that have hornlike or scale-covered skin. Lizards, snakes, and turtles are reptiles.

INDEX

567.9   Amery, Heather
Ame

             looking at --
                    ratops

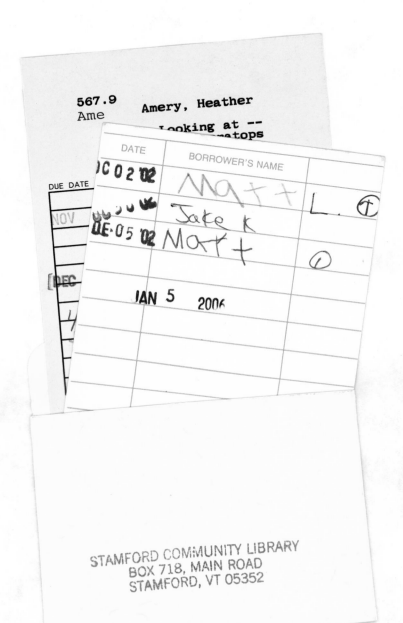

DUE DATE

DATE	BORROWER'S NAME	
NOV		
DC 02 02	Matt	L. ①
	Jake K	
DE·05 02	Matt	①
[DEC		
JAN 5 2006		